HEINRICH MARSCHNER
(1795–1861)

Scottish Songs

Songs to Poems by Robert Burns and William Motherwell

Eight selected songs with English lyrics
for high and low voice

edited by Alexander Aschoff

Bibliographische Information der Deutschen Nationalbibliothek

Die Deutsche Nationalbibliothek verzeichnet diese Publikation in der Deutschen Nationalbibliographie; detaillierte bibliographische Daten sind im Internet über http://dnb.d-nb.de abrufbar.

Impressum

Aschoff, Alexander (Hrsg.):   Heinrich Marschner – Scottish Songs
                                     Songs to poems by Robert Burns and William Motherwell
                                     1. Auflage 2014

Copyright für diese Ausgabe: © 2014 Alexander Aschoff

Herstellung und Verlag: BoD - Books on Demand, Norderstedt

Satz und Layout: Alexander Aschoff

Umschlagbild vorne: »Inverness«; Kupferstich von Appleton, aus: *Picturesque Europe*, New York 1875
Umschlagbild hinten: »Heinrich Marschner«, nach einer Zeichnung von Albert Ludovici,
                                aus: *The Illustrated London News*, August 1, 1857

ISBN-13:   978-3-7386-0259-3

CONTENTS (high / low)

HIGH VOICE

The lovely lass o' Inverness

(R. Burns)

H. Marschner, Op. 103 No. 1

978-3-7386-0259-3

John Anderson my jo

(R. Burns)

H. Marschner, Op. 103 No. 5

Andantino.

1. John An - der - son my
2. John An - der - son my

jo, John, when we were first ac - quent,
jo, we clamb the_ hill the - gi - ther,

your locks were like the ra - ven, your bo - nie_ brow was
and mo - ny a can - ty day, John, we've had wi'_ ane a -

brent;
ni - ther;

but now your brow is
Now we maun tot - ter

978-3-7386-0259-3

My heart's in the Highlands

(R. Burns)

H. Marschner, Op. 103 No. 6

A red, red rose

(R. Burns)

H. Marschner, Op. 103 No. 7

1. My luve is like the red, red rose, that's new - ly sprung in june;
2. As fair art thou, my bon - ny lass, so deep in luve am I;
3. Till a' the seas gang dry, my dear, and the rocks melt wi' the sun,
4. And fare - thee well, my on - ly luve! And fare - thee - well a while!

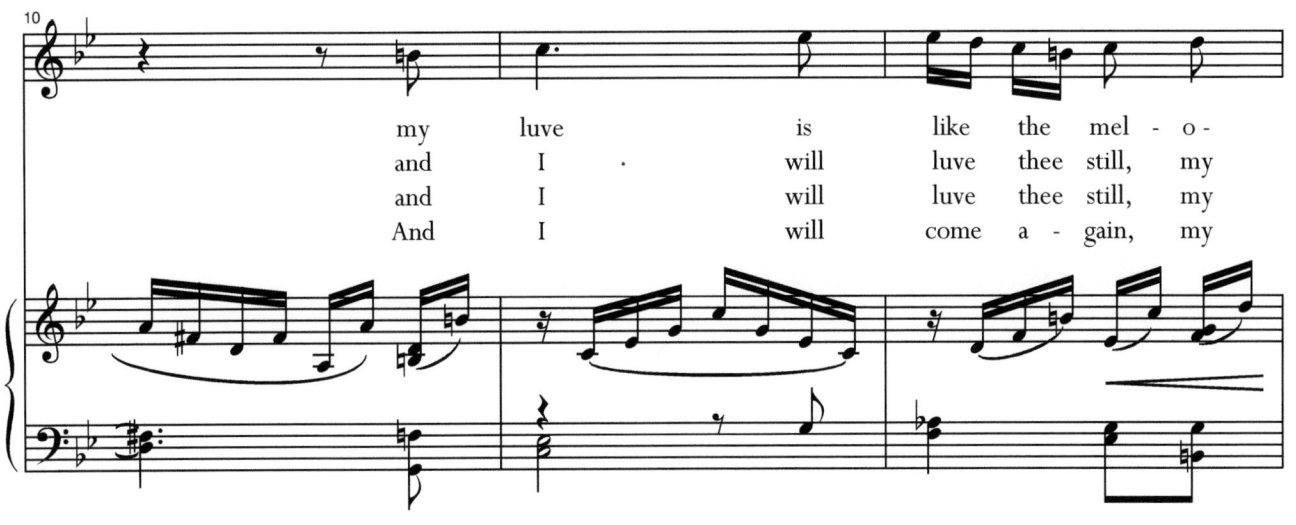

my luve   is   like the mel - o -
and I   will   luve thee still, my
and I   will   luve thee still, my
And I   will   come a - gain, my

die, that's sweet - ly, sweet - ly played in tune.
dear, till a' the seas, the seas gang dry.
dear, while_____ the sands o' life shall run.
luve, though_____ it were ten - thou - sand mile.

978-3-7357-5784-5

Out over the Forth

(R. Burns)

H. Marschner, Op. 107 No. 1

Out o - ver the Forth I

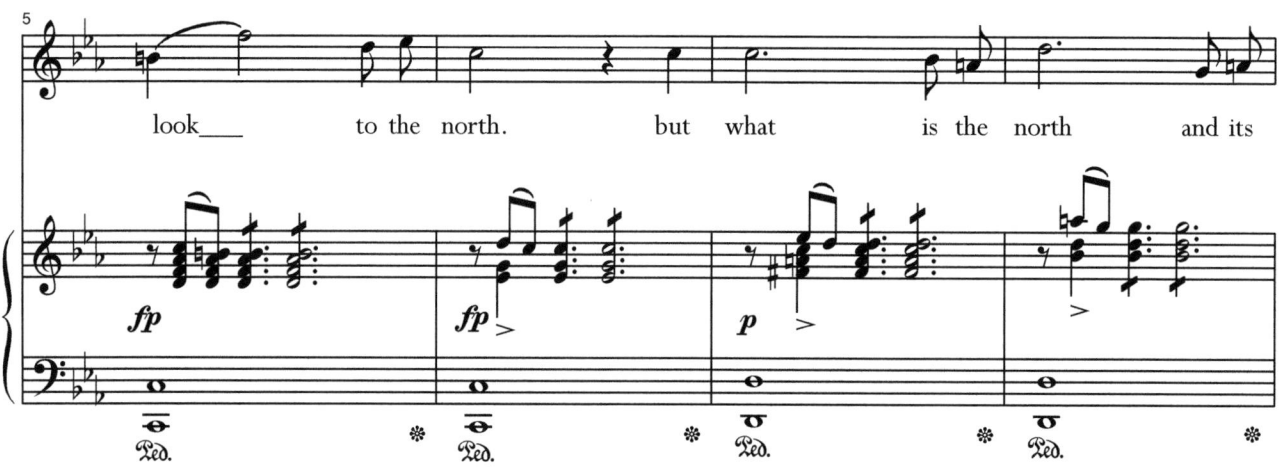

look___ to the north. but what is the north and its

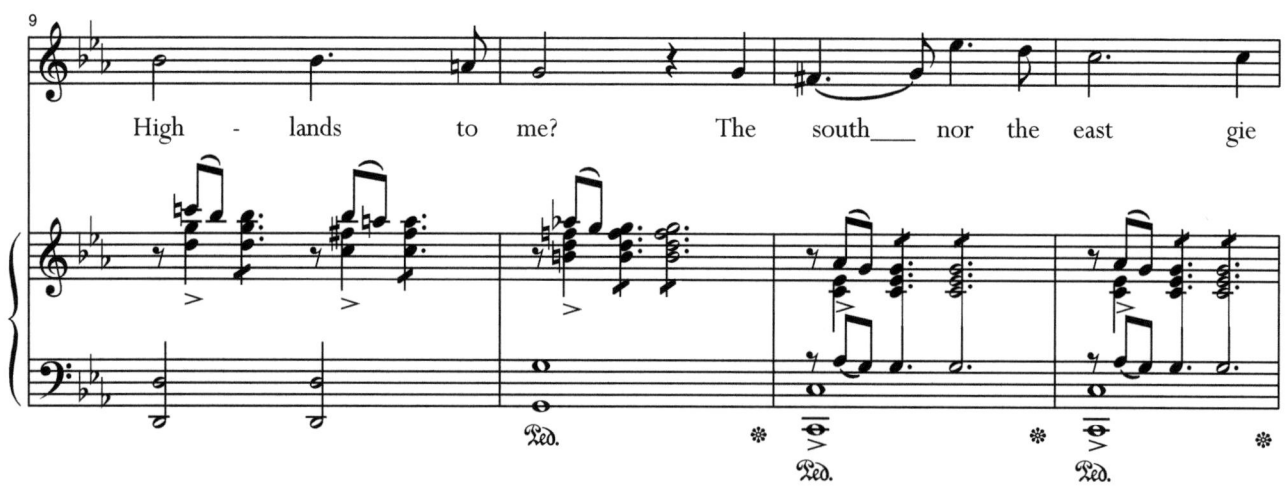

High - lands to me? The south___ nor the east gie

best, the man that is dear to my ba - bie and

me, the man that is dear____ to my ba - bie and

me, the man that is dear to my ba - bie and

me.____

He is gone!

(W. Motherwell)

H. Marschner, Op. 125 No. 3

Molto agitato.

He is gone! He is gone! Like the leaf from the tree; or the down that is blown by the wind o'er the lea. He is fled, the light-heart-ed! Yet a tear must have start-ed to his

eye, when he part-ed from love-strick-en_ me! He is fled, the light-

heart-ed! Yet a tear must have start-ed to his eye, when he part-ed from

lovestricken me! He is

fled! He is fled! Like a gal-lant so free, plumed cap on his

head, a sharp sword by his knee; while his gay fea-thers fluttered, sure-ly

something he muttered, he at least must have ut-tered a__ fare-well to

me! He at least must have ut-tered a fare-well to me! To

me! To me! He's a - way! He's a - way, to far

lands o'er the sea, and long is the day ere home he can be; but

where'er his steed pran - ces, a - mid throng - ing lan - ces, sure he'll

think of the glan - ces that love stole from me?

A - mid throng - ing lan - ces, sure he'll

think of the glan - ces that love stole from me!

poco a poco rit. *a tempo*

From me! From me! He is

gone! He is gone! Like the leaf from the tree; but his heart is of

ritard. *a tempo*

stone if it ne'er dream of me! For I dream of him e - ver: His buff - coat and

Facts from Fairyland

(W. Motherwell)

H. Marschner, Op. 125 No. 5

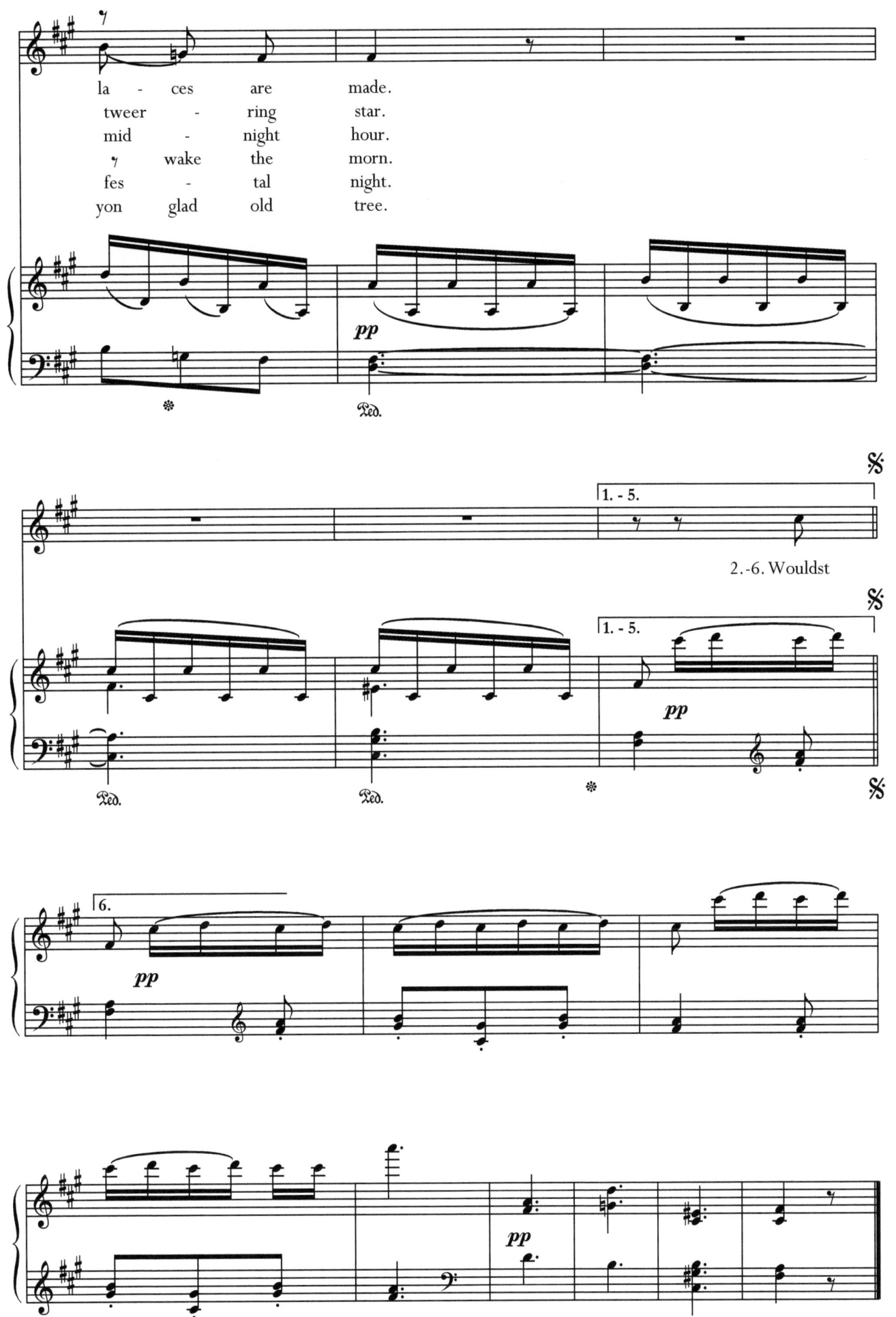

la - ces are made.
tweer - ring star.
mid - night hour.
wake the morn.
fes - tal night.
yon glad old tree.

1. - 5.

2.-6. Wouldst

6.

978-3-7386-0259-3

O were my love yon Lilac fair

(R. Burns)

H. Marschner, WoO

O, were my love yon li - lac fair, wi' pur - ple blos - soms to the spring; and I, a bird to shel - ter there, when wea - ried on my lit - tle wing! How I wad mourn, when it____ was torn by

O gin my love were yon red rose, that grows u - pon the cas - tle wa'; and I my - sel' a drop o' dew in - to her bon - ny breast to fa'! O there, be - yond ex - pres - sion blest, I'd feast on beau - ty

a' the night; sealed on her silk - saft faulds to rest, till fleyed a -

wa' by Phoe - bus' light! Sealed on her silk - saft faulds to rest, till

fleyed___ a - wa'_____ by Phoe - bus' light!

LOW VOICE

The lovely lass o' Inverness

(R. Burns)

(orig. D minor)

H. Marschner, Op. 103 No. 1

fa - ther dear,_____ and breth - ren
ne'er_____ did_ wrong_____ to_ thine_____ or

three,_____ for there____ I lost_____ my
thee,_____ that ne'er____ did wrong_____ to

fa ther dear,___ and lost my breth - ren three._____
thine___ or thee,___ did wrong to thine or thee.«_____

2. Their

John Anderson my jo

(R. Burns)

(orig. A minor)

H. Marschner, Op. 103 No. 5

978-3-7386-0259-3

My heart's in the Highlands

(R. Burns)

(orig. E-flat major)

H. Marschner, Op. 103 No. 6

follow-ing the row, my_ heart's in the Highlands, wher - e - ver I__
e - ver I rove, the_ hills of the Highlands for - e - ver I__
wild-hang-ing woods; fare - well to the tor-rents and loud pour-ing
follow-ing the row, my_ heart's in the Highlands, wher - e - ver I__

go,_____ wher - e - ver I__ go.
love,_____ for - e - ver I__ love.
woods,_____ and loud pour-ing woods.
go,_____ wher - e - ver I__ go.

2. Fare -
3. Fare -
4. My_

Fine.

978-3-7386-0259-3

A red, red rose

(R. Burns)

(orig. G minor)

H. Marschner, Op. 103 No. 7

1. My luve is like the red, red rose, that's new - ly sprung in june;
2. As fair art thou, my bon - ny lass, so deep in luve am I;
3. Till a' the seas gang dry, my dear, and the rocks melt wi' the sun,
4. And fare - thee well, my on - ly luve! And fair - thee - weel a while!

my luve   is   like the mel - o -
and   I   will   luve thee still,   my
and   I   will   luve thee still,   my
And   I   will   come a - gain,   my

die,   that's   sweet -   ly,   sweet - ly played   in tune.
dear,   till   a'   the   seas, the seas   gang dry.
dear,   while_____   the   sands o'_ life   shall run.
luve,   though_____   it   were ten-thou - sand mile.

978-3-7386-0259-3

Out over the Forth

(R. Burns)

(orig. C minor)

H. Marschner, Op. 107 No. 1

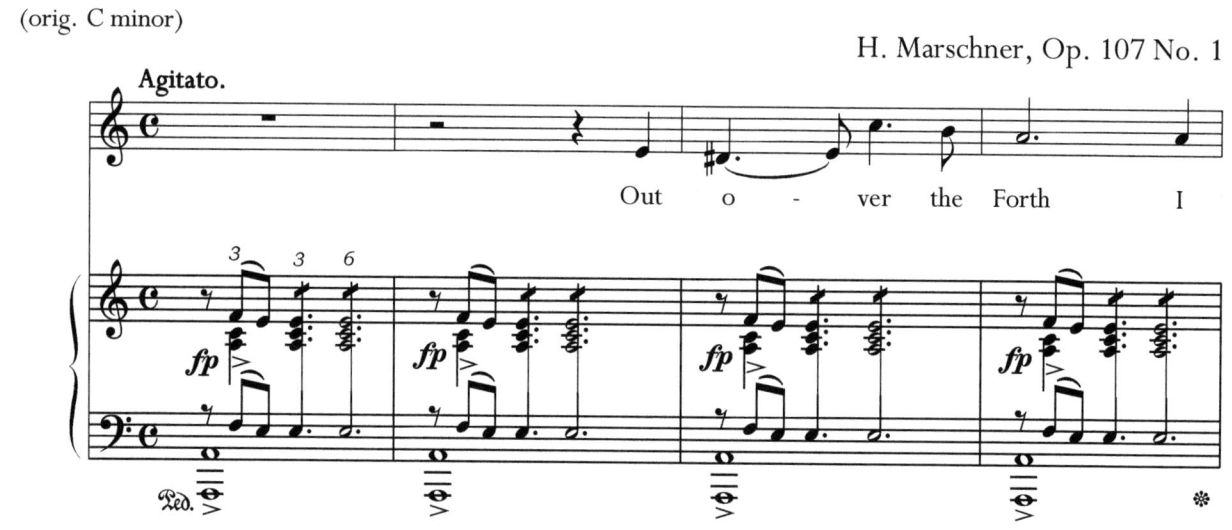

Out o - ver the Forth I

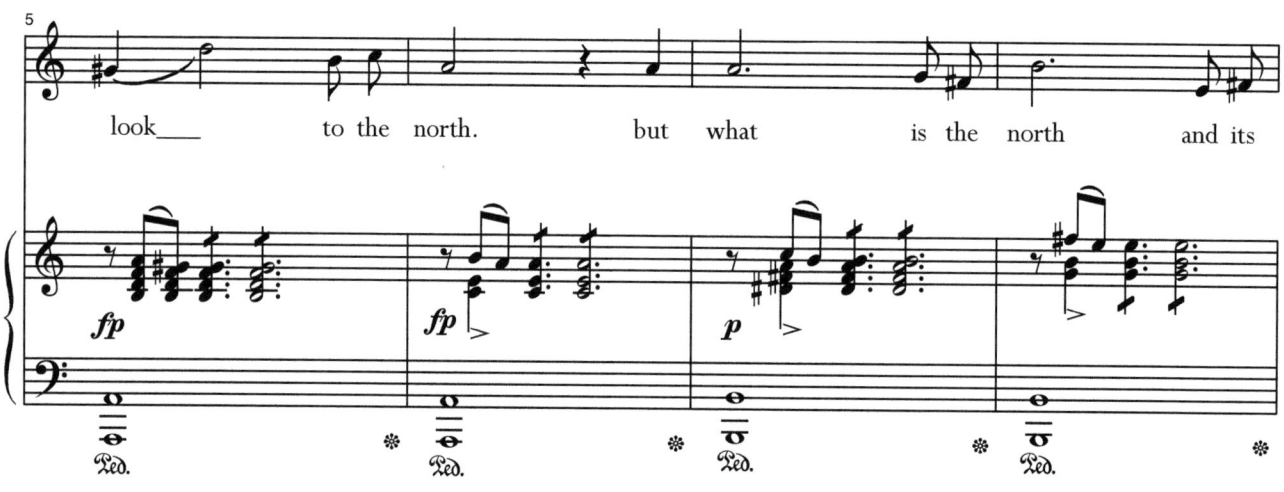

look___ to the north. but what is the north and its

High - lands to me? The south___ nor the east gie

best, the man that is dear to my ba - bie and

me, the man that is dear to my ba - bie and

me, the man that is dear to my ba - bie and

me.

He is gone!

(W. Motherwell)

(orig. F minor)

H. Marschner, Op. 125 No. 3

Molto agitato.

He is gone! He is gone! Like the

leaf from the tree; or the down that is blown by the wind o'er the

un poco rall.

a tempo

lea. He is fled, the light-heart-ed! Yet a tear must have start-ed to his

eye, when he part-ed from love-strick-en_ me! He is fled, the light-

hearted! Yet a tear must have start-ed to his eye, when he part-ed from

love-stricken me! He is

fled! He is fled! Like a gal-lant so free, plumed cap on his

lands o'er the sea, and long is the day ere home he can be; but
where'er his steed pran - ces, a - mid throng - ing lan - ces, sure he'll
think of the glan - ces that love stole from me?
A - mid throng - ing lan - ces, sure he'll

think of the_ glan - ces that love stole from me!

poco a poco rit. .... *a tempo*

From me! From me! He is

gone! He is gone! Like the leaf from the tree; but his heart is of

ritard. .... *a tempo*

stone if it ne'er dream of me! For I dream of him e - ver: His buff - coat and

Facts from Fairyland

(W. Motherwell)

(orig. F-sharp minor)

H. Marschner, Op. 125 No. 5

la - ces are made.
tweer - ring star.
mid - night hour.
wake the morn.
fes - tal night.
yon glad old tree.

2.-6. Wouldst

978-3-7386-0259-3

O were my love yon Lilac fair

(R. Burns)

(orig. E-flat major)

H. Marschner, WoO

O, were my love yon Li - lac fair, wi' pur - ple blos - soms to the spring; and I, a bird to shel - ter there, when wea - ried on my lit - tle wing! How I wad mourn, when it___ was torn by

a' the night; sealed on her silk - saft faulds to rest, till fleyed a -

wa' by Phoe - bus' light! Sealed on her silk - saft faulds to rest, till

fleyed____ a - wa'_____ by Phoe - bus' light!

German lyrics

Die süße Dirn von Inverness

Die süße Dirn' von Inverness
wird nun und nimmer wieder froh;
ihr einz'ger Gang ist in die Mess',
sie weint und seufzt, und sagt nur: O!

»Drumossie Moor, Drumossie Tag;
o bitt'rer Tag, o blut'ges Moor!
Wo kalt und starr mein Vater lag,
wo ich der Brüder drei verlor.

Ihr Lailach ist der blut'ge Klee,
ihr Grab ist grün vom ersten Kraut,
der schmuckste Bursche liegt dabei,
den Mädchenaugen je geschaut!

Nun wehe dir, der du die Schlacht gewannst
und sätest blut'ge Saat!
manch Herz hast du betrübt gemacht,
das dir doch nichts zu Leide tat.«

Ferdinand Freiligrath (1810-1876)

John Anderson

John Anderson, mein Lieb, John, als ich zuerst dich sah,
wie dunkel war dein Haar und wie blass dein Antlitz da!
Doch jetzt ist kahl dein Haupt, John,
schneeweiß dein Haar, und trüb dein Aug;
doch Heil und Segen dir, John Anderson, mein Lieb!

John Anderson, mein Lieb, John, bergauf stiegst du mit mir,
und manchen lust'gen Tag, John, zusammen hatten wir:
Nun geht's den Berg hinab, John,
doch Hand in Hand! Komm, gib sie mir!
In einem Grab ruhn wir, John Anderson, mein Lieb!

Ferdinand Freiligrath (1810-1876)

Mein Herz ist im Hochland

Mein Herz ist im Hochland, mein Herz ist nicht hier;
mein Herz ist im Hochland, im waldgen Revier.
Da jag ich das Rotwild, da folg ich dem Reh,
mein Herz ist im Hochland, wo immer ich geh.

Mein Norden, mein Hochland, lebt wohl, ich muß ziehn;
du Wiege von allem, was stark und was kühn,
doch wo ich auch wandre und wo ich auch bin,
nach Hügeln des Hochlands steht allzeit mein Sinn.

Lebt wohl, ihr Gebirge mit Häuptern voll Schnee,
ihr Schluchten, ihr Täler, du schäumende See,
ihr Wälder, ihr Klippen, so grau und bemoost,
ihr Ströme, die zornig durch Felsen ihr tost.

Mein Herz ist im Hochland, mein Herz ist nicht hier;
mein Herz ist im Hochland, im waldgen Revier.
Da jag ich das Rotwild, da folg ich dem Reh,
mein Herz ist im Hochland, wo immer ich geh.

Ferdinand Freiligrath (1810-1876)

English lyrics

The lovely lass o' Inverness

The lovely lass o' Inverness,
nae joy nor pleasure can she see;
for e'en to morn she cries, alas!
and aye the saut tear blin's her e'e.

»Drumossie moor, Drumossie day -
a waefu' day it was to me!
For there I lost my father dear,
my father dear, and brethren three.

Their winding-sheet the bluidy clay,
their graves are growin' green to see;
and by them lies the dearest lad
that ever blest a woman's e'e!

Now wae to thee, thou cruel lord,
a bluidy man I trow thou be;
for mony a heart thou has made sair,
that ne'er did wrang to thine or thee!«

Robert Burns (1759-1796)

John Anderson my jo

John Anderson my jo, John, when we were first acquent;
your locks were like the raven, your bonie brow was brent;
but now your brow is beld, John,
your locks are like the snaw;
but blessings on your frosty pow, John Anderson my jo!

John Anderson my jo, John, we clamb the hill thegither;
and mony a canty day, John, we've had wi' ane anither:
Now we maun totter down, John,
and hand in hand we'll go;
and sleep thegither at the foot, John Anderson my jo!

Robert Burns (1759-1796)

My heart's in the Highlands

My heart's in the Highlands, my heart is not here,
my heart's in the Highlands, a-chasing the deer;
a-chasing the wild-deer, and following the roe,
my heart's in the Highlands, wherever I go.

Farewell to the Highlands, farewell to the North,
the birth-place of Valour, the country of Worth;
wherever I wander, wherever I rove,
the hills of the Highlands for ever I love.

Farewell to the mountains, high-cover'd with snow,
farewell to the straths and green vallies below;
farewell to the forests and wild-hanging woods,
farewell to the torrents and loud-pouring floods.

My heart's in the Highlands, my heart is not here,
my heart's in the Highlands, a-chasing the deer;
a-chasing the wild-deer, and following the roe,
my heart's in the Highlands, wherever I go.

Robert Burns (1759-1796)

Mein Lieb ist eine rote Ros'

Mein Lieb ist eine rote Ros'
die frisch am Stocke glüht,
eine rote, rote Ros'! Mein Lieb
ist wie ein süßes Lied!

Mein Lieb, so schmuck und schön du bist,
so sehr auch lieb' ich dich;
bis dass die See verlaufen ist,
süße Dirne, lieb' ich dich!

Bis dass die See verlaufen ist,
und der Fels zerschmilzt, mein Kind,
und stets, mein Lieb, so lang mein Blut
in meinen Adern rinnt!

Leb' wohl, leb' wohl, mein einzig Lieb!
Leb' wohl auf kurze Zeit!
Leb' wohl! ich kehr', und wär' ich auch
zehntausend Meilen weit!

Ferdinand Freiligrath (1810-1876)

A red, red rose

O my Luve's like a red, red rose,
that's newly sprung in June:
O my Luve's like the melodie,
that's sweetly play'd in tune.

As fair art thou, my bonie lass,
so deep in luve am I;
And I will luve thee still, my dear,
Till a' the seas gang dry.

Till a' the seas gang dry, my dear,
and the rocks melt wi' the sun;
and I will luve thee still, my dear,
while the sands o' life shall run.

And fare-thee-weel, my only Luve!
and fare-thee-weel, a while!
And I will come again, my Luve,
tho' 'twere ten thousand mile!

Robert Burns (1759-1796)

Im Westen

Ich schau' über Forth hinüber nach Nord:
was helfen mir Nord und Hochlands Schnee?
Was Osten und Süd, wo die Sonne glüht,
das ferne Land und die wilde See?

Aus Westen winkt, wo die Sonne sinkt,
was mich im Schlummer und Traume beglückt;
im Westen wohnt, der mir Liebe lohnt,
mich und mein Kindlein ans Herz gedrückt.

Wilhelm Gerhard (1780-1858)

Out over the Forth

Out over the Forth, I look to the North;
but what is the north and its Highlands to me?
The south nor the east gie ease to my breast,
the far foreign land, or the wide rolling sea.

But I look to the west when I gae to rest,
that happy my dreams and my slumbers may be;
for far in the west lives he I loe best,
the man that is dear to my babie and me.

Robert Burns (1759-1796)

Er ist fort!

Er ist fort! Er ist fort!
Wie vom Baume das Laub,
wie der Flaum, den der Nord
wegführet als Staub.
Er verließ die Geliebte,
eine Trän' aber trübte
wohl sein Aug', als er übte
den Treubruch an mir!

Ach, er ist mir geraubt,
und er zieht in den Streit
mit dem Helm auf dem Haupt
und dem Schwert an der Seit'.
Als sein Helmbusch keck nickte,
war es Reu', die ihn drückte?
Denn sein Aug', o das blickte
zum Lebewohl nach mir!

He is gone!

He is gone! he is gone!
Like the leaf from the tree,
or the down that is blown
by the wind o'er the lea.
He is fled -- the light-hearted!
Yet a tear must have started
to his eye when he parted
from love-stricken me!

He is fled! he is fled!
Like a gallant so free --
Plumed cap on his head,
and sharp sword by his knee;
while his gay feathers flutter'd,
surely something he mutter'd --
He at least must have utter'd
a farewell to me!

Er ist fort, er ist fort,
in die Fern' über See!
Eh' er kehret von dort,
droht mir, ach, noch manch Weh'!
Wo sein Ross er mag lenken,
wo die Lanzen sich senken,
wird der Blicke er wohl denken
der Liebe von mir?

Er ist fort! Er ist fort!
Wie die Blätter vom Baum;
doch sein Herz ist verdorrt,
denkt er mein nicht im Traum!
Denn mir träumt von ihm immer,
und sein Schwert und der Schimmer
seines Panzers wird nimmer
vergessen von mir!

Heinrich Julius Heinze (1811-1860)

He 's away! he 's away!
To far lands o'er the sea,
and long is the day
ere home he can be;
but where'er his steed prances
amid thronging lances,
sure he 'll think of the glances
that love stole from me!

He is gone! he is gone!
Like the leaf from the tree,
but his heart is of stone
if it ne'er dream of me;
for I dream of him ever --
his buff-coat and beaver,
and long sword, oh! never
are absent from me!

William Motherwell (1797-1835)

Kunde aus dem Feenland

Ich soll dir gestehn,
wo wohnen die Feen?
In der grünen Hald,
wo der Mondstrahl kalt
die Blätter versilbert, die Halm' umwebt;
unterm Hügel im Wald
ist ihr Aufenthalt,
und dort ihr kristall'ner Palast sich erhebt.

Ich soll dir gestehn,
was speisen die Feen?
Die würzige Luft,
den Blumenduft,
der weht durch die herrliche Wildnis fern;
Hyazinthen entsprießt,
was die Fee genießt,
beim funkelnden Lichte der zitternden Stern'.

Ich soll dir gestehn,
was trinken die Feen?
Den frischesten Tau,
der im Morgengrau
nur immer die Blüten und Blätter getränkt;
froh schenken wir ein
diesen labenden Wein,
wenn die Stille der Nacht auf die Erde sich senkt.

Ich soll dir gestehn
die Freuden der Feen?
's ist die Jagd, die erschallt
im düsteren Wald,
keck reiten mit Horn und mit Hund wir die Nacht;
über Moore und Höhn,
durch Täler und Seen,
bis vom Klange des Waidwerks der Morgen erwacht.

Facts from Fairyland

Wouldst thou know of me
where our dwellings be?
'T is under this hill,
where the moonbeam chill
silvers the leaf and brightens the blade,
'tis under this mound
of greenest ground,
that our crystal palaces are made.

Wouldst thou know of me
what our food may be?
'T is the sweetest breath
which the bright flower hath,
that blossoms in wilderness afar,
and we sip it up,
in a harebell cup,
by the winking light of the tweering star.

Wouldst thou know of me
what our drink may be?
'T is the freshest dew,
and the clearest, too,
that ever hung on leaf or flower;
and merry we skink
that wholesome drink,
thorough the quiet of the midnight hour.

Wouldst thou know of me,
what our pastimes be?
'T is the hunt and halloo,
the dim greenwood through;
o, bravely we prance it with hound and horn,
o'er moor and fell,
and hollow dell,
till the notes of our Woodcraft wake the morn.

Ich soll dir gestehn,
wie gekleidet die Feen?
In die Fäden dünn,
die den Sommer hin
durch die Kühle des Abends so lustig wehn;
und der Rosenbaum beut
weiches Wams und Kleid,
drin Ritter und Damen zum Feste gehen.

Ich soll dir gestehn,
wenn zum Feste wir gehn?
Schwebt der Mond voll Pracht
in der stillen Nacht
über Land und See, wie ein lieblicher Traum;
dann klingt durch die Luft
Flöt' und Trommel, und ruft
die Fee und ihr Liebchen zum Tanz um den Baum.

Heinrich Julius Heinze (1811-1860)

*Wouldst thou know of me
what our garments be?
'T is the viewless thread,
which the gossamers spread
as they float in the cool of a summer eve bright,
and the down of the rose,
form doublet and hose
for our Squires of Dames on each festal night.*

*Wouldst thou know of me
when our revelries be?
'T is in the still night,
when the moonshine white
glitters in glory o'er land and sea,
that, with nimble foot,
to tabor and flute,
we whirl with our loves round yon glad old tree.*

William Motherwell (1797-1835)

Metamorphosen

O wäre mein Liebchen das Röslein rot,
dort oben auf felsiger Mauer,
und ich, ich fiel ihr, ein Tropfen Tau,
in den Busen mit wonniger Schauer!
Wie wollt ich, weich gebettet, die Nacht
durchwachen im Taumel der Liebe,
eh mich aus duftiger Lagerstatt
der Strahl der Sonne vertriebe.

O wäre sie jener Holunderstrauch
im Lenze bei festlichem Reigen,
und ich, ein Vogel, baute mein Nest
in seinen blühenden Zweigen!
Wie wollt ich trauern, wenn stürmischer Nord
die Blütenzweige zerknickte,
wie jauchzen und singen, wenn junger Mai
mit neuen Blüten sie schmückte.

Wilhelm Gerhard (1780-1858)

O were my love yon Lilac fair

*O were my love yon Lilac fair,
wi' purple blossoms to the Spring,
and I, a bird to shelter there,
when wearied on my little wing!
How I wad mourn when it was torn
by Autumn wild, and Winter rude!
But I wad sing on wanton wing,
when youthfu' May its bloom renew'd.*

*O gin my love were yon red rose,
that grows upon the castle wa';
and I myself a drop o' dew,
into her bonie breast to fa'!
O there, beyond expression blest,
I'd feast on beauty a' the night;
seal'd on her silk-saft faulds to rest,
till fley'd awa by Phoebus' light!*

Robert Burns (1759-1796)